T0035767

SPECIAL DELIVERY

For Freddie, with love
PF

For my dad, Nils-Åke Fahlén,
and for workers doing all kinds of jobs, everywhere
KF

Text copyright © 2022 by Polly Faber
Illustrations copyright © 2022 by Klas Fahlén

All rights reserved. No part of this book may be reproduced, transmitted, or stored in an information retrieval system in any form or by any means, graphic, electronic, or mechanical, including photocopying, taping, and recording, without prior written permission from the publisher.

First US edition 2023
First published by Nosy Crow Ltd. (UK) 2022

Library of Congress Catalog Card Number 2022908644
ISBN 978-1-5362-2985-1

22 23 24 25 26 27 28 APS 10 9 8 7 6 5 4 3 2 1

Printed in Humen, Dongguan, China

This book was typeset in Queulat.
The illustrations were created digitally.

Candlewick Press
99 Dover Street
Somerville, Massachusetts 02144

www.candlewick.com

SPECIAL
DELIVERY

SPECIAL DELIVERY

A BOOK'S JOURNEY AROUND THE WORLD

Polly Faber

illustrated by
Klas Fahlén

It's forty more sleeps
until Jay's birthday.

At a factory far away, everyone is
arriving for a busy day at work.

Something's being
printed, cut, and pressed,

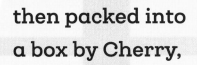
then packed into
a box by Cherry,

moved along a
belt into a crate,
and lifted . . .

into the container on Han's truck.

Han drives through narrow streets . . .

图书馆

and highways.

SPECIAL DELIVERY

He must get to the dock . . .

to reach Chi Wan's gantry crane on time.

The crane is lowered, clamps the container, and lifts it right off Han's truck.

SPECIAL DELIVERY

The container
is hoisted up
and placed into
a slot on . . .

Captain Flip's
enormous ship.

The ship carries five thousand containers, all the same shape and size, but with different things inside.

The crew straps and bolts them into place, then Doug's tugboat guides Captain Flip out of the port to the open sea.

SPECIAL DELIVERY

There's plenty to keep the crew busy while they sail . . .

all the way to
the other side
of the world!

When they arrive,
everyone works
to unload the
containers ...

onto Nate's freight train.
It's very strong and very, very long.

The train travels through the night
to the depot, where . . .

SPECIAL
DELIVERY

DEPOT
1

DEPOT
2

DEPOT
3

SPECIAL
DELIVERY

SPECIAL
DELIVERY

Mack and his reach stacker
move the containers into a
warehouse to be unpacked.

Hannah scans everything to see where it goes next.

Some things are stored.

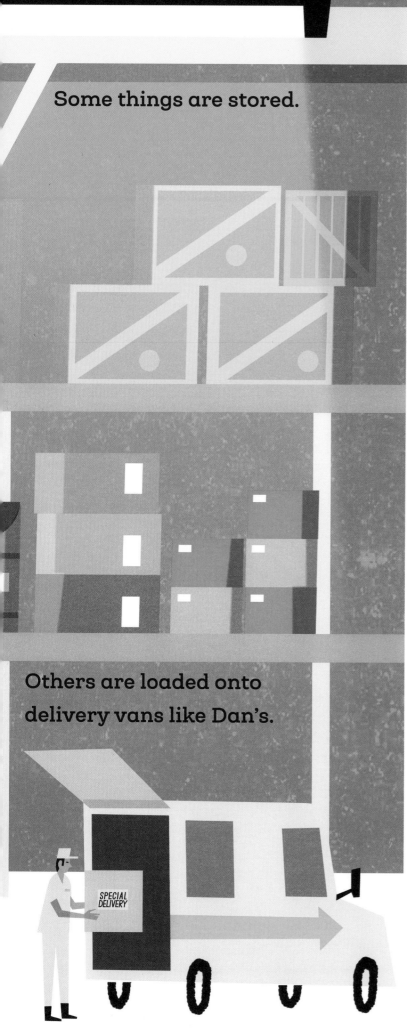

Others are loaded onto
delivery vans like Dan's.

SPECIAL DELIVERY

Dan drives over some hills
to a town,

where he delivers one
box around the back of . . .

Pip's bookshop.

Pip's Bookshop

NEWS

Pip places it in the window
on display. It's spotted by
someone cycling by,

who stops inside to chat with Pip and pay.

Later, she takes her purchase to . . .

the post office.
It's weighed and
stamped by Kofi,
who puts it into a sack . . .

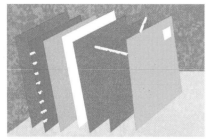
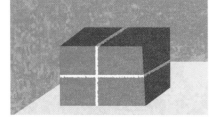

to be scanned and sorted by Porter,

then moved into another sack, for the very last part of its long journey.

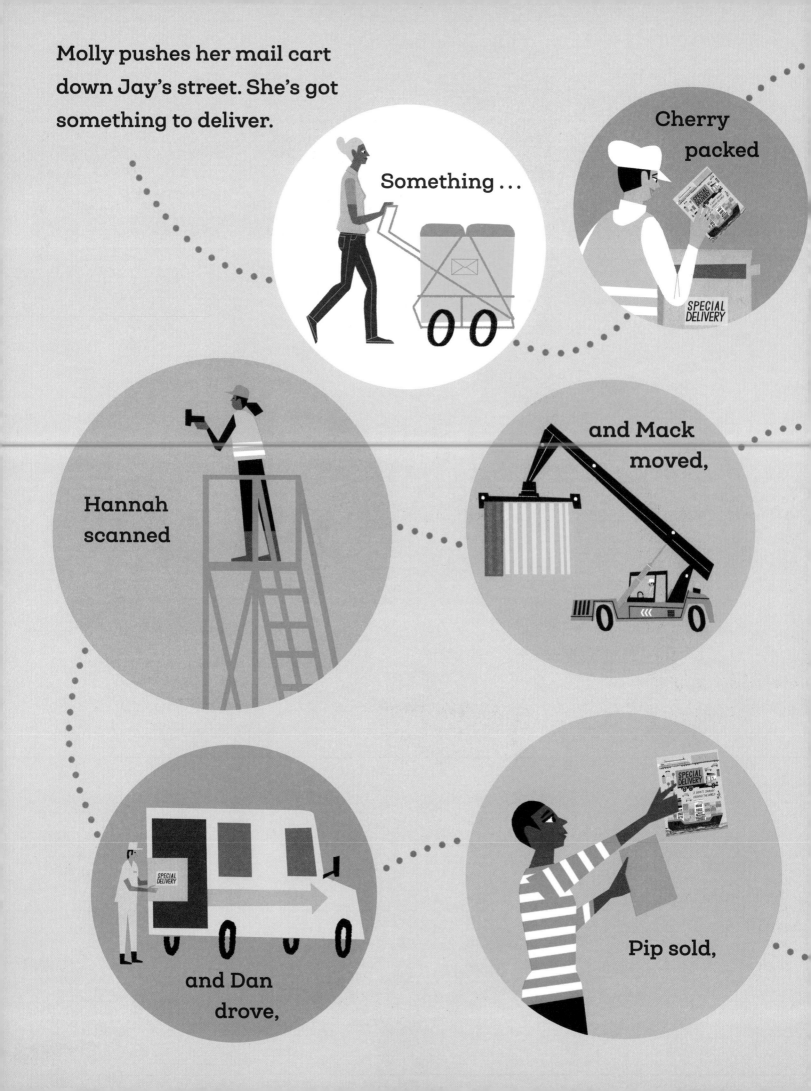

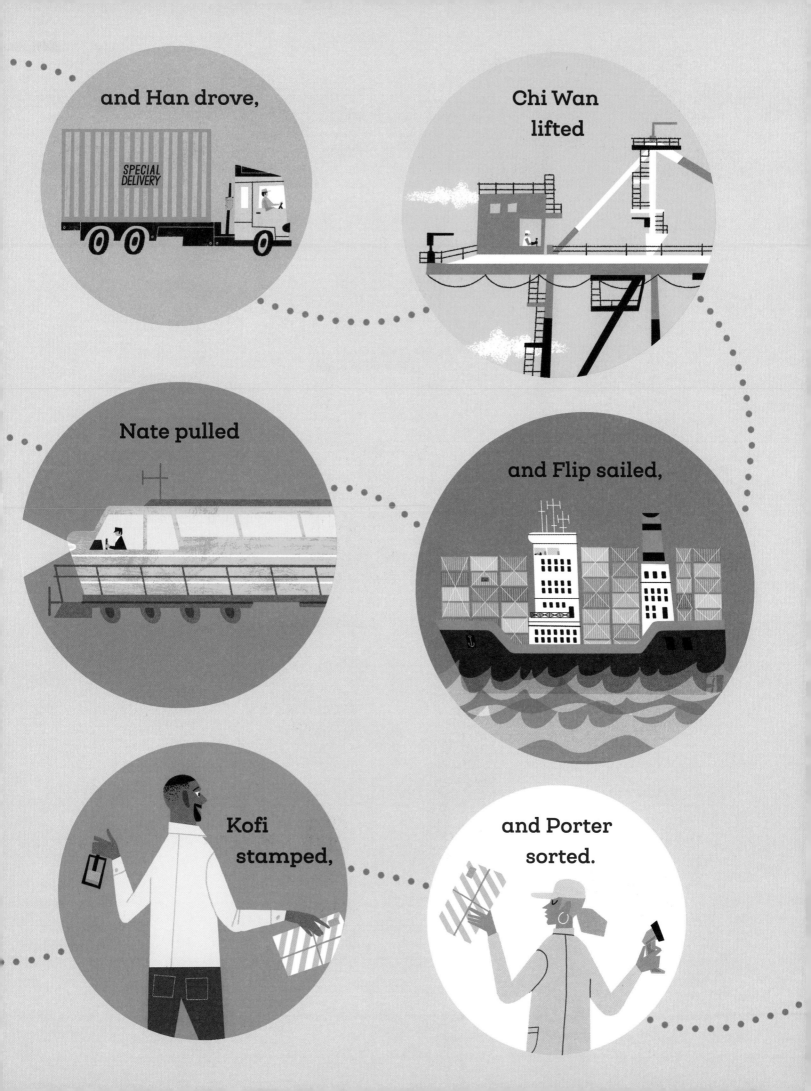

The special delivery is here at last—a present Jay's grandmother chose especially for him.

And he
LOVES it!

Later, Jay has a special delivery for Gran.

But he delivers that . . .

himself!

Special Delivery Numbers

More than **5,000** container ships are at sea on any one day. Around **200 million** containers are moved every year. Many things in your house traveled by shipping container.

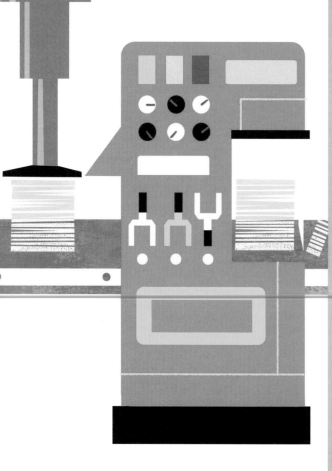

Machines in a book factory can print on **1,300 feet/400 meters** of paper in a minute—that's as long as **10** unrolled rolls of toilet paper!

30 x

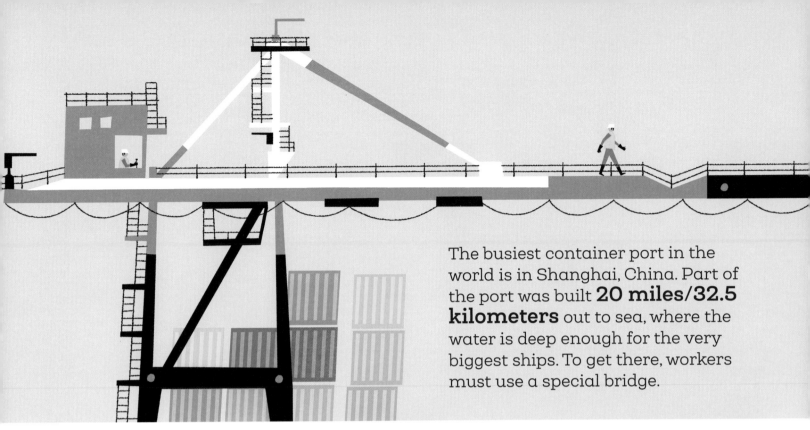

The busiest container port in the world is in Shanghai, China. Part of the port was built **20 miles/32.5 kilometers** out to sea, where the water is deep enough for the very biggest ships. To get there, workers must use a special bridge.

Containers are tied very tightly onto ships, but every year some are lost at sea. In 1992, a container spilled **28,000** rubber ducks and other bath toys. They were still washing ashore more than **15** years later and have been found all over the world.

28,000 x

SPECIAL DELIVERY

The longest trucks in the world are found in Australia. Some can pull three or four trailers at once, so they look like a train on the road. Their loads can be as heavy as **130 tons/120 metric tons**—about the weight of **30** Asian elephants!

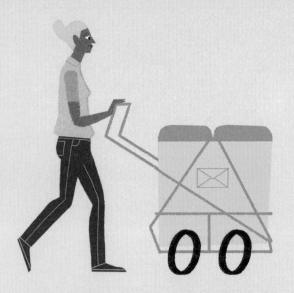

Mail can be delivered to the door of **nine out of ten** homes in the world. (Some people live in places that are too hard for mail carriers to reach.)

There are **more than a billion** bicycles in the world today. In the Netherlands, there are more bicycles than there are people!

Many forklift trucks are powered by batteries. They're programmed to go no faster than walking speed so the people around them are safe. They can carry loads that would otherwise need **100** people to move.

A delivery van driver can deliver up to **200** different items in a single day's work.

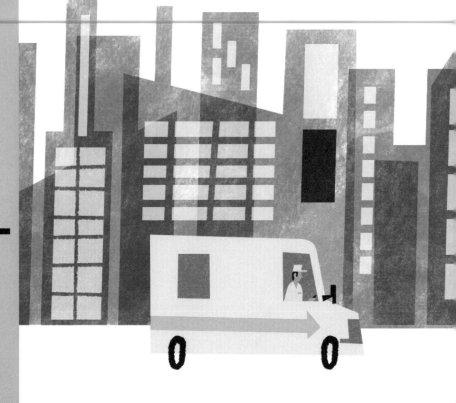

Container freight trains can be **more than 2 miles/3 kilometers** long. One train can do the same job as **several hundred** trucks. That means a lot less traffic on the roads and cleaner air for everyone!